# Peanut Butter & Jelly's Dog Park Adventures

Story by **Wendy Kaupa**
Illustrations by **Brent Plooster**

## ALNI PUBLISHING

To Alexis and Nick - Thank you for all the joy and silliness we shared during our countless hours reading bedtime stories.

For Mom

©2022 Wendy Kaupa
All Rights Reserved. No part of this publication may be reproduced, stored in a retrieval system, or transmitted in any form or by any means—electronic, mechanical, photocopy, recording, or any other—except for brief quotations in printed reviews, without the prior permission from the publisher.
Hardcover ISBN: 978-1-7356895-3-1
Paperback ISBN 978-1-7356895-4-8
Kindle ISBN: 978-1-7356895-5-5

Library of Congress Control Number: 2022914075
Cataloging in Publication data on file with the Publisher.

Illustrations: Brent Plooster
Design and production: Concierge Publishing Services

Printed in the United States of America
10 9 8 7 6 5 4 3 2

It's Dog Park Day!

Every Saturday Mia takes Peanut Butter and Jelly downtown to Misty Meadows Dog Park to see their friends.

As soon as Mia puts her shoes on, Peanut Butter and Jelly get the zoomies and twirl frantically around the room. They are so excited Mia can barely get their leashes attached. "Guys, chill!" she orders.

Once both are leashed, they dart out the door and head to Misty Meadows Dog Park.

On a normal walk, Peanut Butter and Jelly sniff every tree, post, and hydrant. On Dog Park Day, it's full steam ahead.

When they arrive at the entrance, Mack waves. Mack keeps the park neat and tidy.

Mia says, "Hello, Mack."

Mack opens the gate to let them in. He is always happy to see his furry friends and their owners, and Peanut Butter and Jelly wiggle and wag happily. He gives Peanut Butter and Jelly each a scratch behind the ears, and reaches into his pocket for a small biscuit for each pup.

As soon as Mia unhooks their leashes, both dogs take off running around the park. "Have fun boys!" Mia laughs.

Peanut Butter and Jelly spot their best buddy, Gizmo. The three friends begin a game of chase, darting around trees and bushes.

Soon all three are panting and thirsty, so they stop at one of the many water bowls sitting around the park. Peanut Butter spies Mack refilling one of the bowls and runs over for another biscuit.

Jelly spots Hawkeye and darts toward him. Hawkeye is Mack's dog. He comes to the park every week, but he prefers to lie under the shade of an old maple tree.

Peanut Butter trots over to Hawkeye, gives him a quick sniff and tail wag to say hello, and then moseys on his way.

Peanut Butter notices Gizmo and Jelly have joined Mia and her friend Logan. All seem to be paying close attention to something on the ground. Peanut Butter decides to investigate.

Jelly, Gizmo, and Peanut Butter run off to play.

Peanut Butter barks and wags his tail to encourage Ozzie to join the fun.

Gizmo spots it first: a big puddle just past the maple tree where Hawkeye is dozing. Gizmo darts across the park, with the other three dogs hot on his tail. All four dogs leap into the muddy puddle sending a massive splash all over Hawkeye, who wakes up very unhappy.

Peanut Butter, Jelly, and Gizmo joyfully play in the muddy puddle, splashing, barking, and wiggling. Ozzie finds a comfortable spot to nap.

Soon, it is time to go.

Mia calls, "Peanut Butter. Jelly. Time to go!"

Logan yells, "Ozzie. Come here boy!"

"Oh no, what have you two gotten yourselves into?" Mia sighs. "Looks like somebody is getting a bath today!"

He calls, "Ozzie! Ozzie!"

Ozzie is nowhere to be found.

"Hey guys, where did Ozzie go? Is he with Gizmo?"

Mia commands, "Peanut Butter and Jelly, go find Ozzie."

Peanut Butter and Jelly search every corner of the park. They look around bushes, behind trees, and under benches. Gizmo even digs a hole to look! But they don't find Ozzie anywhere.

Finally, Peanut Butter notices Hawkeye and begins to bark. The three friends find Ozzie snuggled up with Hawkeye, both snoozing away.

"You guys did a good deed today! I'm so proud of you. Helping others is always important."

Peanut Butter and Jelly bark happily, "Woof!"

Made in United States
North Haven, CT
30 November 2023